T0067362

THE HEART OF A LEADER

A Thirty Step Guide to Becoming a Better Leader

JENNIFER HIGGINS

ILLUSTRATIONS BY JEREMY JAMES

Order this book online at www.trafford.com
or email orders@trafford.com

Most Trafford titles are also available at major online book retailers.

© Copyright 2008 Jennifer Higgins.
All rights reserved. No part of this publication may be reproduced, stored in a retrieval system, or transmitted, in any form or by any means, electronic, mechanical, photocopying, recording, or otherwise, without the written prior permission of the author.

Print information available on the last page.

ISBN: 978-1-4251-6114-9 (sc)

Because of the dynamic nature of the Internet, any web addresses or links contained in this book may have changed since publication and may no longer be valid. The views expressed in this work are solely those of the author and do not necessarily reflect the views of the publisher, and the publisher hereby disclaims any responsibility for them.

Any people depicted in stock imagery provided by Getty Images are models, and such images are being used for illustrative purposes only.
Certain stock imagery © Getty Images.

Trafford rev. 01/19/2021

North America & international
toll-free: 844-688-6899 (USA & Canada)
fax: 812 355 4082

DEDICATION

I would like to dedicate this book to my family: To my mother, Judy Denham and father, Link Higgins who raised and supported me through all the phases of growing up – the good, the bad, and the weird; and to my sister Pam Olsen, who gave me support and a sparring partner. Now that I'm older and somewhat wiser, I'd like to thank my husband, Ed, and children Zach and Emily, who make life fun and remind me what's really important every day of the year. All of them have loved and supported me throughout this great journey that is life. I thank them all for being who they are and letting me be who I am.

∽

I would also like to thank Melissa Helms for suggesting I write a book, Kathy Ryan and Neal Rickmers for supporting me with ideas, suggestions, and multiple readings of the book, and Lori Marasco for proofing the proof.

∽

Finally, a special thanks goes to illustrator, Jeremy James, for his ideas and support through the "what should the illustration be that makes this concept come to life" period and his dedication and professionalism to providing great illustrations to match the words.

INTRODUCTION

YOU CAN BE a leader regardless of who you are or the job or position you hold. It doesn't take any extra schooling or a fancy title to make you a leader – it takes integrity and character – qualities that come from within. This book is about leading people and how to become more effective at it. In the process of becoming a more effective leader, you'll probably find that you have become a better person. By that I mean, someone who has better interpersonal relationships and who gets better results both in your personal life and your business life. That is because being a true leader means possessing and displaying integrity and character. And people who display integrity and character inevitably have better and more honest relationships with people. True leaders are honest in their interactions and true to their values. That means they're honest and value and respect everyone with whom they interact.

This book is not about the tactics of managing. This book is designed to give you the framework by which you will be in a better position to appreciate and take advantage of what those people you work with have to offer you as a leader and your company in general. Some aspects of what is discussed in this book may be difficult for you to feel comfortable with and assimilate into your way of leading, some may be easy – each person will react differently to each concept, because we all come at things from a different perspective having had different life experiences.

If you are getting this book for yourself – good for you! It means that you believe you can be a better leader tomorrow than you are today and are ready to begin that journey.

If your boss gave you this book, then she sees potential in you and wants you to succeed; so thank her.

If your employees gave you this book, then thank them profusely, because it means that they value you as a person and leader enough to believe that you want to be as good a leader as you can be. It also means that you have created an environment where they feel comfortable saying that – perhaps not so subtly, but the message is there – embrace it and thank them for their belief in you.

This book is not long or hard to read. Each concept or point is made in one page. This isn't about quantity, rather it's about quality. In order to get the most out of this book, you need to read each chapter within each section and then incorporate it into how you think and function as a leader. That may be awkward at first, but the more you "practice" each of the concepts, the easier each will become second-nature, becoming part of how you function without having to think about it. I suggest reading through the book first, then taking each section and each chapter within that section, one step at a time. Just because you read the book, doesn't mean you "get it" or can "do it". You really have to "feel it" and "live it".

Note: As a grammatical convention, I use feminine pronouns.

The Heart of a Leader
30 Steps You Can Take to Become a True Leader

THE HEART OF A LEADER

A Thirty Step Guide
to Becoming a Better Leader

Section 1

You

THE FIRST SECTION is all about you. If you want to be a true leader, you need to start by looking at yourself and how you function and think. Some of the things in this section are going to seem touchy-feely or "new age" to some. If concepts about feeling good and communicating well are uncomfortable for you, I recommend just reading through the material and trying to "digest" what's being said and the points being made enough to know that they apply to everyone. We're all human, with strengths and weaknesses. Either you're reading this book because you want to be a better leader or you've been "directed" to read this book by someone who exerts some influence over you. Either way, I can guarantee you that there are things you can take from each and every chapter that will make you a better and more successful leader.

So, even if something feels uncomfortable or "hokey" to you, just try it, knowing that there are many others who feel the same way. As long as you are honest as to who you are, you will maintain your integrity as you build character.

Section 1

YOU

Chapter 1

BE OK WITH WHO YOU ARE!

BE OK WITH who you are, knowing that you will continue to learn, grow and evolve your whole life, whether you want to believe it or not. Understand that every step that you took up until this point, brought you to this exact moment – so don't regret what you've done or what you are or second guess yourself! Realize that everything you do today gets you to tomorrow!

What you want to start focusing on is evolving. What that means is really looking at the things that aren't serving you as well as you'd like, and deciding to work on changing or modifying those behaviors to better suit what you want to get out of a situation or life. For example, something that I've worked on my whole life is being honest. Now, I'm a very honest person and always have been. However, some would say that I am honest to a fault because I tell people what I think when they ask for my opinion or if I think they need to hear my version of the truth. What I've learned over the years, though, is that I don't want to be so honest or so brutal with the truth that I lose my audience – after all, what's the point, if you're trying to make a point, and no one's listening! So what I have worked on and continue to work on is finding a way to make my point without turning my audience off so that they're not listening. It's been a long, hard road and it's a life-long journey for me, but one that I continue to work on. I didn't like the results I used to get, so I decided to change. I like the results better as I continue to refine and get better at not losing my audience, so I continue to work on changing!

This book is meant to be about learning new ways of doing things – it is definitely NOT about beating yourself up for not being perfect or not "doing things right". Everything contained in this book is meant to help you be a better leader. Be genuine, honest, and sincere as you "try out" these new skills and concepts. Try them in small steps if they feel awkward, until you get your bearings and you feel more comfortable with the "new you". It may also help if you can enlist some of your staff or your friends to help you by telling them what you're trying to accomplish, so they better understand the changes you're going through. Share with them the concepts you're working on and see if they can help by encouraging you when you're doing it better than before. They can also help by prodding you back on the right path if you stray from your intended target.

However you decide to work on these changes, be yourself and be OK with whatever stage you are at – it's all part of the evolution that is learning new skills and changing for the better.

Bottom line: Be OK with who you are right now, knowing that you will continue to grow and change. Maintain your integrity throughout the process of building character.

Chapter 2

YOU ARE NOT IN CONTROL!

YOU ARE NOT in control – Accept it and move on! I don't care how much you think you are – YOU ARE NOT IN CONTROL! There is only one thing you can control and that is YOU – and even that is probably hard for many of us sometimes! The quicker you come to the realization that you can only control yourself and how you respond to situations, the quicker you can move forward with creating a positive environment and growing and evolving yourself. Now, let that sink in for minute.

In the work world, you cannot control your staff, your coworkers, or your boss – at best, you can only encourage them to behave the way you want them to. Within your family, you cannot control your relatives – even though you probably wish you could at times. As a parent, you cannot control your kids. Even if you can control some aspects of people's lives, you cannot control them or what they think or feel, so don't even waste time on thinking you can or should. Just move forward knowing that you are the only one you can control. You can control what you think, how happy you are, how you interact with people, even what kind of day you're going to have! And if you think about it, that's a very powerful and liberating reality!

As soon as you let go of any energy you're putting into controlling others, you can focus that energy on controlling yourself.

1. Control your temper so that you don't lose it.
2. Control your reactions to people and situations so that you ensure those reactions are positive and get positive results.
3. Control your tongue and your words so that they get positive results through praise and productive interactions.
4. Control your thoughts so that you think positive thoughts and minimize or eliminate negative thoughts.
5. Control your body language and posture so that you send positive, unspoken messages.

Bottom line: You cannot control anyone but yourself and you should spend your energy focusing on controlling the 5 points above.

Chapter 3

IF YOU SCREWED UP, ADMIT YOUR MISTAKE AND APOLOGIZE!

IF YOU SCREWED up, admit your mistake and APOLOGIZE! Apologies go a long, long way in EVERY situation – Yes, even at work! The one thing you must make sure of is that the apology is heartfelt and honest! If you've made a mistake or hurt someone's feelings, or been a jerk (and you know you've done all three of these at least once in your career!) then learn how to apologize. It's very simple, just a few words – "I'm sorry for ……"

Make sure your apology is heartfelt. You don't want to negate the apology by making it be the other person's fault. "I'm sorry that you misinterpreted my words," is not an apology – it's blaming the person you're trying to apologize to and not taking the responsibility yourself! Instead, saying something like, "I'm sorry that I said something that hurt your feelings – that wasn't my intent," makes it an apology. The point of any apology is:

1. To acknowledge to someone that you have hurt her in some way.
2. To allow the person you've hurt to move forward by releasing any anger or resentment she's holding onto toward you.
3. To allow the relationship to grow and strengthen.
4. To admit you're human and that you made a mistake.

There is nothing you have done now or in the past, that cannot be apologized for. And it really doesn't matter if the person "forgives" you as that may take time – the point is that you apologize and mean it.

You'll be amazed at how much energy people put into being angry or holding grudges based on not getting an apology. In the work world, that equates to energy that IS NOT going into positive production or thought – so even if an apology seems "touchy feely" and not something that belongs in the workplace, think of it as something that will help you get better results – because, ultimately, it will.

Examples of work-related things that could and should be apologized for:

1. Calling someone out in a group – in this case, you should privately apologize to the one you embarrassed first. Then you should apologize to the group for embarrassing someone in public. Remember, every person present at the original incident was probably embarrassed for the person being called out and lost some respect for you as a result of your actions.
2. Not letting someone talk or finish her thoughts.
3. Not accepting someone's ideas in a positive way.
4. Accusing someone of something she didn't do.

Bottom line: Apologize and mean it when you have made a mistake, hurt someone's feelings, or been a jerk.

"Thompson I apologize! I thought I had disconnected that ejection panel.
When you started talking about a raise I got nervous and pushed it out of habit."

Chapter 4

You can VISIT Pity City,
but you're not allowed to MOVE there!

YOU CAN VISIT Pity City, but you're not allowed to MOVE there! It's very easy to feel sorry for your-self when you're a leader and things aren't going well. Perhaps your boss has yelled at you for some-thing you or your staff did or didn't do, or your results aren't what they were forecasted to be – you fill in the blank! It's also very easy to turn that to anger towards your staff. So, if you need to feel sorry for yourself, do it privately, and then get over it. The really important thing is to be aware when you're down and headed toward Pity City and remove yourself from circulation until you're done moping. Remember, the only thing you can control is you and your reaction to people, situations, etc. In this case, by you creating a negative atmosphere for yourself, you are sending that message to your staff too. You'd be amazed at what they believe is the cause when you're down. Maybe there's layoffs coming, or your spouse is leaving you, or you got yelled at by the big boss and they're all in trouble! I can guarantee you they'll imagine far worse things than the real truth. The point is, don't ever underestimate the power that a leader has over her staff's emotions when she is "down in the dumps". Your staff will spend time and energy trying to figure out what's wrong with you, which is time and energy they could or should be spending on productive work. In the end, as the leader, you set the tone for your team.

I'm not saying you can't be down or that you have to walk around with a goofy grin on your face all the time, but if you have to be depressed or "pissy" or grumpy, do it somewhere away from your staff and get it out of your system. Then come back into circulation and get the positive juices flow-ing again. See Chapter 2 and remember that the only thing you can control are your emotions and your reactions to things – so you can choose to move on and get on with your day and get back to business whenever you want to!

Bottom line: If you need to feel sorry for yourself, do so privately and get over it quickly and then get back to the business of your business. (Note: See Chapter 6 on being grateful if you want to turn around your attitude quickly.)

Chapter 5

WE'RE ALL HUMAN!

WE'RE ALL HUMAN – we make mistakes, we cry, we bleed, we get scared, we get anxious, and sometimes, we even get things right! What this really means is this – give everyone around you, including yourself a break. Cut everyone some slack. Everyone makes mistakes because they're human, so get over the fact that no one is perfect. Let people make mistakes and then move on. Let yourself make mistakes, apologize if you've hurt someone, then move on.

The more accepting you are of yourself, the more accepting you'll be of others. Maintain a reasonable sense of the "gravity of the situation". The vast majority of mistakes are not life and death, or even that big of a deal in the grand scheme of things. The big deal that gets made of them is usually because they made someone or a group or company look bad. Understand that most negative things that people do are based in fear. Many people spend their whole lives being afraid and this makes them look out for themselves and sometimes do mean or deceitful things to others. I'm not excusing the behavior, just providing a bit of explanation for it – and for many of us, understanding why someone did something helps us forgive, let it go, and move on. In your own case, many of the things you do now, that don't serve you well, may be based in your own fears.

You will ultimately find that people are more alike than different. Most everyone wants to make a decent living, be treated with respect and dignity, understand where she fits in the company, and be respected for the job she does and the person she is. The great part is, every one of those things is free except the decent living part – and that's what the company takes care of. If you, as a leader, can provide the free things, people will respect you and like working for you, and ultimately do a better job for you and your company.

Bottom line: Realize that we're all human and cut your people and yourself some slack.

Chapter 6

BE GRATEFUL!

THINK OF THE things you are and can be grateful for: your life, your health, your loved ones, your friends, your pets, your house, your faith, your job, your intelligence, your sense of humor, your ……you fill in the blank. Start every day by being thankful for all the things you have. Don't dwell on what you don't have, dwell on what you DO have. The point of this is to ensure that you don't focus energy on what is missing from your life, rather focus energy on what is good about your life. You'll find that you start each day stronger and better if you focus on what you have and are therefore grateful for. This focus also helps give you perspective throughout the day and can especially help if you're beginning to feel sorry for yourself (see Chapter 4).

So don't take your life or each day for granted. Learn to appreciate and savor the wonderful things in your life – from the people you love at home to the people you work with to the nature around you, to anything that makes you happy about being alive. It helps keep all the little things that go "wrong" throughout the day in perspective and makes you a more well-rounded person.

At work, when someone brings you a problem, be grateful that she had faith in you to help solve the problem. When someone tells you something that she knows you're not going to want to hear, be grateful that she felt you should know and made you aware. Be grateful that you work with people who want to do well, succeed, and be part of successful company.

Bottom line: Be grateful for all the good things you have in your life. This can help you balance your perspective throughout the day and will help you stay grounded.

Chapter 7

LIFE IS FUN AND FUNNY!

LIFE IS FUN and funny! If you're not having fun and seeing the humor in life, then you need to regroup! If you're dragging yourself into work every day, ask yourself why? I don't mean, because you need the money…we all need to make a living, instead ask yourself, "Why am I spending energy being miserable?" Then ask yourself, "Why don't I spend less energy being negative and more energy being positive?" It takes a lot of energy to be negative – you actually can get energy from being positive. Happiness is a choice – Remember that! Work and the workplace should be fun. People work harder and are willing to give it their all if they also have fun. They can give more of their "all" because having fun recharges people's batteries – while not having fun will actually drain them and you of energy.

If you're a sourpuss, you'll have sourpusses working for you. And sourpusses spend a lot of time and energy maintaining that attitude and making sure those around them stay that way. If you're positive and have fun at work, you'll have a positive, fun team working for you. Imagine the power of having you and your staff using positive energy throughout the day, and even smiling and having fun. You spend way too many hours each day working to not have fun at it. In fact, we spend 33% of the day at work – so try smiling and being positive and see what positive results you get. You'll find that you have more energy and more time for doing good things – positive things. I can guarantee you that by turning around your attitude, you'll notice that your life gets better, and you'll also turn around your staff and they'll help the company's bottom line. Don't worry if it takes people some time to get used to the "new you" – they'll like it much better and you'll like what you get back in return!

Bottom line: Life is fun and you spend less energy and get better results in all aspects of your life by being positive and having fun.

Chapter 8

ASSUME THE BEST!

ASSUME THE BEST means exactly that – Always assume the best – in people, situations, and in life! Always assume the best! Make that be your screen saver or hang it up on your wall so you can see it all day so it can remind you to "Assume the Best." Disregard the saying, "When you assume, you make an ass out of you and me." That is based on negatives. Assume the best moves you to a positive mode of action.

How many times have you assumed the worst? A lot I bet, because it seems to be human nature. And has it ever been the worst? Probably not! So, rather than take the negative tact, take the positive approach and assume the best. This holds true for people and situations. If something doesn't sound right, assume the best and go to a credible source for some more information. If something sounds bad, assume there is something you're not being told or not aware of and try to find the whole story. There is ALWAYS a credible explanation and it's NEVER as bad as you think or when you let your assumptions take their natural course – to their worst-case conclusion.

You'll be amazed at how much better things go at work with your staff when you assume the best. Imagine asking someone on your staff about something in a positive way rather than grilling her assuming you already know the answers and they're all negative. Imagine saying to your boss that you trust your people and you'll get an answer and explanation rather than throwing someone or yourself under the bus as a human sacrifice because you assume the worst. Imagine hearing something that doesn't sound right and going to the source to get the real story – I assure you, the "source" will be relieved that you came to ask for the facts rather than running off problem-solving or blaming or "shooting" without all the facts, because you assumed the worst, or didn't assume the best.

The point is, you get much better results when you assume the best because you instill trust and respect in your people. They begin to realize that you'll come to them to get the facts rather than just take everything you hear and going to the negative with it. They'll trust you and be willing to go further with you down the road to success for themselves, for you, for the team, and ultimately the business.

Even if you find out something is worse than you had hoped, by assuming the best and gathering facts and trusting people, you'll be able to fix or work through the problem much quicker because you assumed the best rather than went to worst case scenario and worked back from there – guaranteed – every time.

Bottom line: Assume the best in people, situations, and in life and you will find that the results are always easier to deal with and your people have trust and respect you more as a leader.

Chapter 9

ADMIT WHEN YOU DON'T KNOW THE ANSWER OR DON'T UNDERSTAND SOMETHING!

ONE OF THE most liberating things in the business world is to be honest and secure enough to say when you don't know the answer or don't understand something. To think that anyone knows the answer to anything and everything they're asked about in a given day is ludicrous. But many people, leaders included, believe they should have all the answers. So, when asked something they don't know the answer to, they either lie, make something up that sounds plausible, or dance around the issue enough so as to divert attention away from the fact that they don't know the answer. Worse still, leaders who don't know and won't ask, end up making decisions based on bad information. Don't fall into that trap!

If you don't know the answer to something you're being asked, say that you'll get the answer – and then go out and get it. You may be being asked by someone who believes you should have the answer, and quite possibly you should – AT YOUR FINGERTIPS. A good leader either knows the answer or can get the answer quickly (that's at your fingertips). You don't have to waste valuable brain space on something you can get the answer to quickly by looking it up or checking with someone who has that expertise or knowledge.

Similarly, if you don't understand something, don't nod your head like a ninny and assume you'll catch on at some point. Hard as it is to believe, not everyone is clear in speaking in public or one-on-one! At a reasonable point in the conversation or presentation, stop the speaker and ask for clarification. If you're in a meeting with others, when given an opportunity, ask clarifying questions. I can assure you, when you ask the question, you WILL NOT be the only one who didn't understand! People may even come up to you later and secretly thank you, confessing that they didn't understand what was being said either!

Another positive that will come of this is that your people will be more willing to say they don't know rather than pretend they do. In the end, you'll gain respect from your staff and peers for admitting you don't know as you gain knowledge and understanding from asking for clarification.

Bottom line: Admit when you don't know the answer and ask for clarification when you don't understand something.

Section 2

YOUR TALK

THIS SECTION IS devoted to communication. That's because you can boil just about all issues, problems, and misunderstandings down to communication, or more specifically, poor communication. There is no one who cannot benefit from honing her communication skills, so make sure you don't underestimate the important lessons here.

There are those who would have you believe (and you might be one of them) that communication is more of that "feel good" stuff. Well, you know what? They're right – it is feel good stuff. And what's wrong with that? At the end of the day, just about all anyone wants to do is feel good. If you can provide an environment where your employees feel good and you feel good, guess what. They like where they work, they trust their leader, they like what they do, they want to do a good job, and they are more productive. So even if you're purely "in it for the money", there's money to be made in making people feel good and you can do that better by being a better communicator.

Good communication is the foundation of everything at work and in life – relationships, teamwork, partnerships, trust, feeling valued – you name it! Even if you don't believe it right now, take it on faith as you read the chapters in this section that better communication will improve all aspects of your work life. And like most other aspects discussed in this book, good communication will most assuredly improve your personal life too.

Section 2

YOUR
TALK

Chapter 10

SHARE YOUR PERSONAL PERSPECTIVE AND EXPERIENCE

SHARE YOUR PERSONAL perspective and experience – it makes you real! This is very hard for some – to share a part of themselves with coworkers and employees, but the more you can show people that you're human – the more willing they'll be to go the distance for you, the quicker they'll come to your rescue when you need it and the quicker they'll dismiss bad rumors that can be flying around.

As an example, when I have to talk to someone about coming on too strong with her coworkers, I share that I am on a life-long quest to soften and tailor my "honesty" message so that I don't lose my audience. That results from having come on too strong with people when I was younger and first managing and learning that once I lost my audience, my message didn't matter because it wasn't being heard and that I certainly wasn't leading. By telling someone my story, I have made it more human by putting myself in her shoes. For the receiver, it makes it easier to "digest" the message because someone else has experienced something similar to what she is struggling with. You can call it "misery loves company" or better stated, "people feel better knowing someone else has gone through something they're experiencing".

The more you share yourself and your experiences, the more human you will become for your employees. And believe it or not, many employees have trouble seeing their leader as human. It's similar to how you probably felt the first time you saw a teacher outside of the classroom. It was hard to imagine that she shopped for groceries just like a normal person did! When your employees see you as more human, it means that they will be more apt to listen with compassion and understanding to what you say, will be more willing to trust you and believe you, will be more willing to tell you the truth, and will be more willing to dismiss negatives about you or possibly bring them to your attention so that things can be addressed.

Bottom line: It's important for your employees to see you as human. The more of yourself that you can share through personal experiences and your perspective, the more human you will be in their eyes.

Chapter 11

ANALOGIES HELP MAKE POINTS

ANALOGIES HELP MAKE points, break things down, and make them less complicated. Analogies are one of the most effective communication tools that there are because they give your listener a mental picture of what you're talking about. Using analogies in your speech or in conversation makes you much more interesting to listen to – which gives you a more attentive audience when you talk.

Here's a simple example of an analogy. If you're talking about being a clumsy dancer, you can simply say, "I'm a clumsy dancer." You've stated your point, but you haven't "painted a picture." But, what if you said, "I dance the way a Winnebago parallel parks!". Now your whole audience is mentally picturing themselves at the wheel of a Winnebago, trying to parallel park it! Whether or not they've ever driven a Winnebago, or parallel parked for that matter – they have a mental image of what it would be like to parallel park a Winnebago and can laugh at the image that conjures up of your dancing. By using analogies, your story, speech, pep rally, or conversation is richer and people will remember the analogy and what you've tried to convey.

In a work environment, here is a true example where an analogy got a point across in a very vivid way. I was part of a team working on a project rolling out a software program on a very large scale. We were in the early stages, and most of us were very naive about how much time, energy, and human power was needed in order to do the many tasks needed to make each aspect of this roll-out successful. Luckily for us, there were several seasoned veterans on the team, who had done project work of a similar scale to what we were working. When we were faced with a particularly daunting chunk of work with an even more daunting deadline, one of those seasoned folks said, "You know, you can't make a baby in one month by having nine women pregnant at the same time!" WOW, did that stop everyone in their tracks! Why? Because we'd all been struggling with the management-directed timeline that if we threw enough manpower at this particular task, we could get it done in a shorter period of time than those of us living the reality knew to be possible. With those few words, we were able to make the point that the tasks we were working were linear and therefore could not be done concurrently – even if we had 100 men – or 9 women! Now, don't think for a minute that management gave us a huge break on the timeline that was unrealistic, but we were able to make them understand that the tasks were linear rather than parallel, and that allowed us enough time to get enough done to make the deadline.

Bottom line: Analogies are a great tool that make your communication more vivid and help make points.

Chapter 12

YELLING DOESN'T ACCOMPLISH ANYTHING

YELLING DOESN'T ACCOMPLISH anything! Most people don't even hear the words you're saying when you're yelling. There is no place for yelling at work, or anywhere in your life for that matter – but let's concentrate on work for now. Yelling is your reaction to something, and unless you're yelling for help, DON'T DO IT. You may think that yelling gets people's attention, or makes your point more clear, but it DOES THE EXACT OPPOSITE. I can tell you from personal experience, when someone is yelling at you, you are not hearing the words – you're actually physically and emotionally trying to protect yourself. When you're yelling, the words you're saying are not being heard or understood or processed in a rational way. More importantly, respect for the yeller is diminished or obliterated completely.

Yelling at someone actually does the following:

1. Demonstrates the yeller's inability to communicate effectively.
2. Diminishes the yeller's credibility and respect from anyone involved.
3. Creates an environment where the person you're yelling at, and any others who hear it or hear about it, work in fear and diminished productivity.
4. Creates an environment where others will feel sorry for and/or come to the aid of the person being yelled at – even if the person being yelled at is in the wrong or is a less-than-competent co-worker.
5. Damages whatever relationship the yeller may have had with that person and any others who hear the yelling or hear about the yelling second or third hand -- and they will! This kind of behavior travels quickly and far in the rumor mill.
6. Means the yeller has to apologize before she can do anything else or move forward with that person and any others who hear the yelling or hear about it.

There are no positives that come from yelling at someone at work, only negatives. You diminish your credibility with that person and anyone else damaged by your outburst, either by her directly witnessing it or indirectly hearing it through a wall or having it repeated to her by the recipient of your anger, or someone else who heard it through the wall or was told the story. Can see the wildfire spread?! Not only do you burn the recipient of your anger, but anyone standing nearby gets burned as do those who get to see the charred remains and scarred and scorched earth left in the wake of the fire your yelling creates. It may take all the character and integrity you can muster to stop yourself from yelling, but that's what you need to do to be a leader.

Bottom line: Yelling produces only negative results. If you feel like yelling at someone, get by yourself to cool down until you can collect your thoughts and communicate rationally.

Bill puts on his trusty "Silent Suit" while Mrs. Foster
reviews his quarterly sales figures.

Chapter 13

BELITTLING PEOPLE DOESN'T ACCOMPLISH ANYTHING

BELITTLING PEOPLE DOESN'T accomplish anything other than diminishing your credibility. If you ever wanted to diminish your own credibility while at the same time diminishing someone's productivity, belittle someone. By belittle, I mean say something that is mean or mean-spirited about her – either a physical, personal, or cultural attribute. Kids do this all the time. Children at a very early age pick up on differences and point out those differences, sometimes, in not so nice or subtle ways. As they grow and are trying to exercise their dominance over others, they point out those differences in order to make themselves feel better by making the one they're belittling feel worse. It sounds silly or petty when described this way and it's easy to point to children who don't know any better, or are learning and haven't experienced the full circle of teasing. But, when adults do it, it's really hard to understand – but it happens, and the damage is real and far-reaching.

There is absolutely no reason to make comments about another person that pertain to her personal appearance or body, her clothes, education, ethnicity, background, religion, speech or accent – NOTHING PERSONAL! If you do, you are less than the bully on the playground – less than that bully because we can excuse children for not knowing how to behave appropriately all the time, but you're an adult. And as an adult, you need to have the character and integrity to communicate in a positive, professional way. Belittling someone can never be a part of that.

If you think this doesn't happen at work, I'll share an experience I had. I worked with a woman from a European country. She had met an American man, fell in love, married him, and moved to the States. Her English was very good, albeit with a northern European accent. Because she did not grow up in the states, there were some idioms and references that she didn't understand. When she didn't understand something, she was very good about asking for clarification because she was always striving to perfect her English. One day, our boss was angry about something and said that perhaps her heritage was causing her to react the way she was reacting. Her interpretation to the comment was that because she was a "foreigner" she didn't behave properly. She never trusted him after that incident because of the hurt it inflicted. She felt that if he was going to belittle her that way once, he would do it again and that he was not a fit boss to have her working for him. To approach this professionally, he certainly could have said, "I don't understand why you're reacting this way to my request to redo this work", but instead he chose to point out that she was culturally different, and that perhaps, that accounted for her inappropriate (implied) reaction to his request. Had he chosen this approach, he could have retained a very talented and productive employee. Instead his ill-chosen words cost him both her credibility and everyone else's respect in the office, who heard about the comments – because the story of the belittling spread like wildfire and the message was loud and clear – if he did it to her, he'll do it me – Think about that and choose your words carefully.

Bottom line: There is never a reason to say something that is mean or mean-spirited about someone's physical, personal, or cultural attributes.

Translation: "Look Xanther, I'm sure on Rittel 7 you folks might do things a certain way, but us Othinions here on Teggius 5 don't give a snark about that!"

Chapter 14

ALWAYS ERR ON THE SIDE OF OVER-COMMUNICATION

WHEN DEALING WITH your staff, always err on the side of over-communication. Or said another way, "When in doubt, spell it out!" You must remember that you have had many more conversations and thought much more about things that are important to you than your staff ever could have, so what may seem perfectly clear or obvious or overkill to you will not be so with your staff. And even if you're "sick" of talking about something, your staff probably hasn't heard or discussed one tenth of what you have on any given issue.

Give people updates and information about what's going on. You'll be amazed how they respond when they feel they are "in the know" and are being kept up-to-date on things that affect them. Did you know that one of the most important things that employees surveyed identified as being extremely important to them, is to be "in the know" on what's going on? So, just because you've "thought" about something for weeks on end, or had so many meetings about something, that even if you think you're over-communicating, to your staff you're not! Even if it's something they've heard once, it doesn't hurt to hear it again as they may have a different perspective and more information now than when they first heard it.

Also, in sharing information, make sure you leave room for asking questions. Those questions are sure to open up areas that are unclear to others and will allow for that much more communication. For your employees, there is really no such thing as over-communication from you.

Finally, sending your staff a powerpoint slide show or presentation that goes to senior management without discussion or explanation of what it is and how it was received, doesn't count as communication. Make sure you share what's going on and going up the ladder, but include the details of what was asked for, what was presented and how it was received.

Bottom line: When in doubt, over-communicate. Even if you're sick of discussing something or think it's resolved, your employees may be hearing it or understanding it for the first time.

Section 3

Your People

IF YOU DON'T believe that your people are your most valuable asset in business, then stop right here and rethink your position. Because you will never get as much from your people or get as far in business as you can and will once you understand that your people are the bedrock on which all of your success and ultimately your company's success is built. I don't care if you're selling penny candy, cleaning office buildings, or building the greatest software known to humankind, there is nothing that gets done in business that doesn't have a human being attached to some part of it. So, as a leader, your job is to understand that your people are your most valuable asset and then let the rest of your job and their jobs flow from there. Interestingly enough, I've heard many managers, trying to be leaders, lament the fact that they have to "spend so much time with and on their people". What did they think their job was going to be as a leader?!

This section will help you understand the concept that your people are the basis of everything your company is and everything you do as a leader. They are not an interruption to your job – THEY ARE YOUR JOB!

Section 3

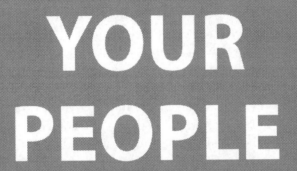

YOUR PEOPLE

Chapter 15

YOUR PEOPLE ARE ALL YOU HAVE!

WHAT WOULD YOU do if all of a sudden, all your staff resigned – right now. Do you think your business would survive? Oh sure, there are some business that are automated and could limp along for a while, or some that would have a residual that the pain might not be felt for a while, or you could hire new workers – but who's going to train them? The bottom line is that all business ultimately is done by human beings, and the better you treat those human beings and value them for being the bedrock of your business, the better off your business, and you, will be!

Do not ever believe that company value is all about "share-holder equity", or the price of stock, or sales. It's all about the people who do the work that makes the stock have value in the first place! Any company that talks about the most important thing being stock price and shareholder equity has missed the entire foundation for their business being in business. Because without your people, I don't care if you're selling a product or a service – WITHOUT YOUR PEOPLE YOU HAVE NOTHING! People are not interchangeable, disposable commodities. It is, and always will be about your people, so you should do anything you can do to keep those people happy and productive and employed.

There are some "hard costs" every business incurs in employee turnover. Advertising and training cost money. What's less obvious, but even more costly are the "soft costs". Those are the things like the amount of time and energy it takes to sift through resumes and applications, and then refining that list to the few that you want to talk to. There's the time it takes to interview and pare your list down to the one you want to make a job offer to. There's the time it takes to get a new employee through orientation for the current employee doing the orientation. There's the time it takes your best employee to put together a training plan for the new employee, and the time it takes your best employee to train that new employee – because during the time that she's developing the training plan and training the new employee, she's not able to do her work! In fact, by some estimates, it costs 200% of an employee's salary to fully replace her. So employee turnover is more costly than just the obvious hard costs and should be something you avoid.

Of course there are those times when a job or company isn't the right fit for an employee. Those partings can be clean and professional. But by understanding that every one of your employees has part of your company in her head and has some history to share, everyone that leaves, takes a part of your company with her. Every new person that you hire takes a while before she learns that history and becomes a productive part of your culture.

Bottom line: Don't ever think your business will survive without your employees – when you boil it down, they're really all you have. Your people are your most valuable resource – hands down.

Chapter 16

TRUST IN YOUR PEOPLE – ALWAYS!

TRUST IS A really hard concept for some, because it means making yourself vulnerable. Rather than trust being second-nature to many, it's like a foreign concept. Trust is really all about treating your employees like intelligent adults and probably how you would like to be treated – remember that when in doubt.

1. Trust is hardest to establish when you need it the most
2. Trust is a two-way street – do not expect your employees to trust you if you don't trust them
3. The vast majority (I'm talking 99% here) of employees do not try to do a bad job or do something dishonest without a reason – like not being trusted or treated like an adult

If you've ever worked somewhere where there was trust – and a lot of people can honestly and sadly say they haven't – you know that even the less-than-honest minority are kept in check by the vast majority of folks that like to be trusted. Those folks make sure that anyone that is out to undermine that trust is kept on a short leash so the trust is maintained by the individuals on the team itself. On the other hand, many places have enough "security" and "safety measures" built in so that even really good and honest employees feel like they're being spied on and slip closer to "the dark side" than they would if they were in an environment of trust. Create or maintain an environment where your employees don't feel trusted and see how many ways they find to screw you, your business, your reputation, your bottom line – you fill in the blank. Because people will find very clever ways to make a company "pay" for not trusting it's employees – simple things like taking home office supplies all the way up to fraud and embezzlement. Now, I'm not for a minute suggesting that some jobs (like those that handle money) don't need to have safeguards in place, they absolutely do. But they should be there as much for the employees' protection as for the company's protection and the employees should know and understand the safeguards. But for many other parts of the working world there does not need to be someone looking over people's shoulder or trying to find ways to entrap them. All that does is create an environment where even honest employees can find "the dark side". See Chapter 8 and "Assume the Best" and trust your people.

Bottom line: Work to implement an environment of trust where you trust your employees and they will work to keep that trust.

Chapter 17

EVERYONE IS ENTITLED TO HER OPINION – AND IT'S RIGHT BECAUSE IT'S HER OPINION!

THE DEFINITION OF an opinion is:
> noun – a view, judgment, or appraisal formed in the mind about a particular matter.

Therefore, EVERYONE has, and is entitled to her opinion on anything and everything. The best part about an opinion is that you get to be right, because it's your viewpoint of the world! That goes for everyone! So don't fall in the trap of either telling someone her opinion is wrong or asking someone for her opinion and then disagreeing with her. Both tactics fail leaders every time – guaranteed!

When someone expresses her opinion, she is simply stating her view of that particular subject matter. You can THINK she's right, wrong, crazy, silly – you fill in the adjective – but here's an alternative to consider: What about thanking her for her opinion and then considering it like you would anything else that you consider throughout your workday.

You'll be amazed the results you get by thanking someone for sharing her personal viewpoint on something. First of all, sharing your opinion takes courage in many workplaces. By asking for and respecting someone's opinion, you are simply getting someone's perspective on something and usually getting another's perspective helps you see things that you may not have seen or anticipated. It is a very good workplace where people have different opinions that they are willing to share and are valued for those different opinions. Groupthink is not good – look at the Challenger disaster if you want a tragic example of that process as well as management not listening to the opinions of those with the expertise. Encourage an environment where individual's opinions are shared and respected. You'll find that problems are solved more creatively and quickly when you have fostered and support that kind of work environment. Because your people are free to share their opinions on things, they will feel respected and be more willing to share each and every day – you'll get the best out of them and they'll want to continue to give their best.

As a leader, you should be seeking out those who are willing to share their opinions and treating them like gold. Having people who will keep you informed on their version of the truth helps you be a better leader because you have more than just your own perspective. You can't be all places at all times, so having those different perspectives gives you that much more information. You may be able to better handle small, medium, or even big problems by seeking out and listening to opinions.

Bottom line: Everyone has opinions, which are their version of their truth and all are correct because it's their version. Seek out and value those employees who will share their opinions as it gives you different perspectives and more information when making decisions.

Chapter 18

EVERYONE IS DIFFERENT
AND NEEDS TO BE TREATED DIFFERENTLY!

A LOT OF people talk about treating their workers the same. However, as a good leader, what you should really strive for is treating each person the way she needs to be treated to bring out the best in her. To be the best, you need each of them and the different perspectives each brings to your business. There are entire courses and books on how different people function – everything from Myers-Briggs personality testing to "love language" religious training – you can certainly spend a long time in this area and should consider it as part of team-building. It helps each person understand how her coworkers see the world and how best to communicate with each other.

Understand and believe that everyone you hire has something to offer your company. Your job as a leader is to create an environment where everyone's opinion is valued and where all employees realize that each of them is an important part of the company. This takes some doing, because many companies perpetuate an environment where employees are pitted against each other or taught and rewarded to find ways to show how they're more important than others in their group. You can counter this by creating goals that must be met by everyone in your group performing at their best. Everyone has something to offer, and the more flexible you are in your approach with your staff, the more each of your people will feel free to be herself. This will help each of them release their positive and creative energies for you and your company's benefit. So don't assume because someone is different and doesn't approach things the same way you do or the same way another employee does that she isn't valuable. It's up to you to make sure that everyone knows that everyone is valued and needed, to make the team and the company succeed.

In order to bring out the best in every one of your people, you need to treat them each in a way that they will understand what you're saying and asking and will receive your praise and constructive criticism in a productive way. For example, some people crave the limelight and love having their name up on recognition boards, while praise for another may be a privately delivered, heartfelt, thank you. Make sure the praise and the constructive criticism fits the person's personality so she'll really hear and appreciate your message.

You also want to make sure you create an environment of acceptance that allows and encourages employees to value each other's differences and differences of opinion. This has to start with you as the leader and which can then cascade through to your staff. This will help them understand that they are each important to the company and will foster open communication, idea-sharing, and problem-solving.

Bottom line: It's helpful to know your people well enough to ensure that your praise and constructive discussions with her are productive. Understand that each of your employees brings value to your team – value those differences and make sure your employees value each other's differences.

Chapter 19

TELL YOUR EMPLOYEES HOW GREAT THEY ARE!

EVERYONE WANTS TO be praised for doing a good job. Make sure that you find ways to tell your employees what a great job they're doing. That doesn't only mean that every quarter you have a meeting and tell the group they're doing great – you should do that too – but find ways to individually tell your employees they're doing a good job in a way that is meaningful for that employee – remembering that some want recognition in front of the group, some want it privately, and some may not really care how they get it – but want it none-the-less.

One of the best things you can do is catch an employee doing something right. That's a bit of a foreign concept for most of us. We do it with children all the time – "good job" or "great effort" or "nice teamwork" or "keep up the good work". We give kids gold stars and pats on the back for a good effort – and why? We do it because we want to reinforce good behavior and encourage more of it. So why don't we do that with adults? Maybe we're afraid if we praise someone, she might think we're "soft" or we think that she'll get lazy, but human nature dictates, if you want more of a certain behavior or outcome, catch someone doing it and praise it so that she understands what she's doing right and will do more of it !

Quick note of caution: Don't end your praise with a "but":

- You did a great job this quarter, **but** we need to do better next quarter.
- You did a great job this quarter, **but** we didn't win group of the quarter.
- You did a great job, **but** you aren't going to be able to keep this up.

Make sure that your praise ends with praise and doesn't wander off into what isn't going well or that it won't last. The "what we need to do is keep this up or turn things around even more" can come at some other time. Instead, praise your staff as often as you can.

Bottom line: Catch your people doing great things and praise them for it – as much as you can!

Chapter 20

COACH YOUR EMPLOYEES TO SUCCESS!

EVERYONE NEEDS TO come out of a situation with a way to succeed and have her dignity intact. This is a critical point when dealing with your staff as a part of conflict resolution and coaching. Ultimately, you want to ensure that the person has a way to succeed and come out of the situation with her dignity intact. This produces a win for you and a win for her. Ultimately, what you want to do is coach your employees to success, not out the door. Everyone needs to believe she can succeed, turn a negative around, and retain her dignity throughout the process.

Many times, during the administration of a performance appraisal or coaching session, you, as the leader, end up "breaking someone down" whether you mean to or not. Your employee may not have expected the message you had to deliver, and if there were negatives, she may very well have not have heard all you had to say or the way you said it – even if you tried to be honest and positive. Hearing unflattering or negative things about yourself is difficult. So make sure that you, as the leader, preserve her dignity and at the same time, stay with her and make sure she is going to be able to regain her composure and go back out and face her coworkers. Ultimately, though, you must believe your employee will succeed and make sure she knows that. If you don't believe it, then your lack of belief will come out in words, gestures, tone, or body language – but, she'll know it's only a matter of time before she's out the door.

Coach your employee to success:

1. Believe that your employee will succeed and get back on track.
2. Ensure that you reiterate good points along with the "negatives" and constructive criticism.
3. Make sure the employee understands that you want to help her to succeed and will do everything in your power to help her get back on track.
4. Remember she's not going to hear all the words or process the content exactly as you are giving it – make sure she repeats back the important points she needs to do to get back on track and that she understands you believe she will succeed.
5. Assess whether or not she's OK at the end of the session to go back to work – she might need time to regroup – maybe time alone in your office – offer her time and space to regroup.
6. Check in with her later on to make sure she's OK and that she understands you're there to help her.
7. You will probably need to regroup the next day with the employee, once she's had time to process the message. Ensure she can reiterate what she has to work on and reinforce your belief that she'll succeed.

Bottom line: Believe in your employees and that they can turn things around. Coach your employees to success.

Chapter 21

ENCOURAGE YOUR PEOPLE TO SPEAK UP AND SPEAK THE TRUTH!

ENCOURAGE YOUR PEOPLE to speak up and speak the truth. For many leaders, hearing the truth is really frightening, or worse yet – they think they're hearing the truth, but they're not! Some would rather insulate themselves from the truth, or punish those that speak the truth (their version of it, that is!) and brand them as malcontents or non-team-players. As a true leader, you want to have a work environment that encourages your people to speak up and speak the truth so that things that are going wrong can get fixed and things that need attention, get attention. If you don't encourage the truth, you'll have people lying, or letting things happen that they know are wrong or not in the company's best interest because they're afraid of the consequences or because they think no one will listen and nothing will change. IT HAPPENS ALL THE TIME! And when you ask employees why they didn't or don't speak up, they say:

1. I tried, but no one listened.
2. Are you kidding! I did that once and got labeled as a malcontent!
3. No way! I'll get told I'm not a team player again and it'll show up on my review!

Now I'm sure you're shaking your head in affirmation, because we've all heard and experienced this. What's important is that to get the best out of your employees, you need to create an environment where anyone can "push the stop button" to stop production when she sees something is not right. That's the only way to ensure that quality work – whether it's a product or a service – is being done and waste isn't taking over. Listen for the truth in what your employees say. It isn't always what you want to hear but it's what you need to hear the most! What you want are folks that will challenge the norm and speak the truth. Encourage your employees to speak up and speak the truth and THANK THEM when they do. Make a GOOD EXAMPLE out of those that speak up. You'll have to use some of your best communication skills and make sure that your body language doesn't scream "I don't want to hear this!" when someone has the courage to tell you the truth, because it's usually not easy to hear. Remembering that it is someone's opinion and therefore her version of the truth can make it easier to listen to. And listen to it you must, because some of the best ideas and most telling comments come from those closest to the job! Assume the best and go out and try to validate the information you're hearing.

If you don't encourage people to speak the truth and reward them for it, you'll get what many companies have – an environment where people avoid answering or lie because they don't want to suffer the consequences of telling the truth. If you think the truth hurts, imagine the cost of the lies! Encourage your people to speak up when they see something going wrong or have a suggestion for doing something better. You'll foster an environment of empowering your staff that is unstoppable and unbeatable.

Bottom line: The truth may not be easy to hear, but you need to hear it. Encourage your staff to speak up and speak the truth when they see something that needs attention. Thank them for being honest and speaking up.

Chapter 22

MAKE YOUR PEOPLE FEEL IT IS SAFE TO MAKE AND ADMIT MISTAKES!

MAKING IT SAFE to make and admit mistakes is probably one of the hardest things to "teach" anyone. This is because we're taught from a very early age, in school and at home, not to make mistakes. Making mistakes costs you grades and teacher, parental, and coach approval. So it might take some work to get to the point where you can be OK with making mistakes and admitting to making mistakes. But, both skills are worth it – and here's why. When you make a mistake, it has several benefits:

1. You learn in a visceral way, what not to do in the future, in a way that reading about it or hearing it from someone else can never do for you.
2. You learn to take risks that will allow you to make bigger leaps forward than you can ever make if you're taking slow and overly cautious steps because you and your team are afraid of making mistakes.
3. You learn to recognize when something isn't going right quicker than if you have to keep going with something that isn't working because you "can't make a mistake" or worse yet, admit you made a mistake.
4. You foster an environment of productive risk-taking that allows breakthroughs in teamwork, productivity, process-improvement – you name it, that is not possible when everyone is protecting themselves and their team from making a mistake.

Some of the greatest inventions, intellectual and creative breakthroughs, and business and team successes are a result of mistakes made. The real lesson in this is, "How were the mistakes handled?" Was someone fired and made an example of or was the person or team allowed to acknowledge the mistake, decide what to do to "fix" it and then given the space and time to do just that – fix it.

I worked for a company that was rolling out desktop computers and a new network system to its staff. It was a huge monetary investment as well as a huge staff and training investment because it was going to take everyone away from their job for several days as the system was rolled out and training took place. There would also be reduced productivity for several weeks as everyone got used to the new way of doing business. Not long before the "big rollout", an announcement was made that the rollout would be delayed. Someone with some backbone had stood up and said that the system really couldn't be rolled out as it was – so the rollout was delayed until the system problems were fixed. I don't know whether or not someone was fired over that (I'd like to think not) but was always impressed and grateful that someone had the integrity to say that something wasn't ready for primetime even though it was admitting a mistake – because it saved countless hours of missed productivity and ultimately, customer dissatisfaction for the company.

Bottom line: Mistakes get made all the time in business. Create and foster an environment where people aren't afraid to make mistakes and admit it and are able to make them safely and learn from them and move forward.

BUSINESS REALITIES

THE FOLLOWING ARE some business realities that you need to be aware of and some things you can do to make your workplace better. Both should help you on your way to being a better leader. Some of these realities will be frustrating to you, and some may seem silly or stupid. You can sit and be frustrated about them and bemoan the fact that you had no idea that this is what being a better leader was all about, or you can pull yourself up by your bootstraps and work on getting better each day at dealing with them – I suggest the latter.

If you've mastered some of the previous skills and concepts, then dealing with these realities will be all the easier, because they are merely outcomes of how most businesses have evolved and therefore how employees behave in order to cope. Each of the realities will be easier to implement or change as you master the skills you've been working on from the first three sections.

Remember, these are the outcomes of your work's culture and your attitudes and the environment you've created as a leader. All of it can be changed for the better if you want it to and are willing to do the work necessary to make those changes happen!

Section 4

BUSINESS REALITIES

Chapter 23

SEEK OUT OPINIONS FROM YOUR STAFF BEFORE YOU EMBARK ON CHANGES

SEEK OUT OPINIONS before you embark on changes. Regardless of the size of the change you're contemplating, get people's opinions and ask them how they'd do it. You especially want to engage the opinions of those doing the job or with first-hand, on-the-ground knowledge. The folks on the ground almost always have good suggestions about making things better. This gets buy-in from those that need to do the work necessary to make the changes and is half the battle when implementing changes. Whenever you're making a change and trying something new, you'll initially get resistance from some – that's normal. If you can get half your people excited about the change, that's huge, because people don't usually buy into something until they see how the change will benefit them – and even then, it can be a hard process. If you've included them in the process, though, even if you don't use all their ideas (as long as you've validated them and listened to them) the fact that you've sought out their opinions will go a long way to getting their support.

Once you've made the changes, be willing to modify things along the way if you see something is not getting the desired results. Throughout the process, seek out feedback and support those courageous enough to give opinions and speak out! The road to success is not always straight, so you may have to do some zigging or zagging. While you don't want to make a change a day, you do want to get input and feedback along the way. Thank those willing to speak up and tell you the truth about how things are going. Ask them what changes they would make to bring about the necessary corrections. The support you'll get from your team for taking into consideration their input and opinions will be invaluable. It will also foster more honesty and feedback and that is exactly what you want and should encourage.

Bottom line: Seek out your people's opinions and give them the opportunity to help craft changes on the front end. Seek out their honest feedback and input throughout the change process.

Chapter 24

Make the goal a vivid picture in everyone's mind

One of the most important things for any team is to understand what the goal is that they're all striving for. Whether it's a 99% quality ratio, or answering 400 calls per hour, or $1,000,000 worth of sales – if everyone doesn't see and understand what the goal is, then they're not going to be working towards the same results or "rowing in the same direction" to get to that goal. It is absolutely critical that your company's goals are reflected in its leaders' goals, which should then be reflected in each leaders' employees' goals. In the mid-1960's someone asked a janitor at NASA what his job was. He said, "To put a man on the moon." Talk about alignment of goals!

It may be hard to believe that all goals wouldn't be in alignment within a company, but I can assure you it happens all the time. For example, how many times has the marketing side of the house had different and even conflicting goals from the customer service side of the house? Without aligned goals, both sides may not see how they have to fit and work together and therefore should have shared or aligned goals.

It also may be hard to believe that everyone on your team doesn't "see" or "live" the goals the way you do, but it happens all too frequently. As an example, I worked for a company that distributed hair care products to hair salons. The warehouse manager had just gotten the product inventory to match the computer system inventory. At that time, the customer service folks that I was leading were still taking orders on paper, only entering them into the computer later on, when they had time. This resulted in having to call back customers to tell them of product shortages, etc. while requiring the double work of taking the order on paper then entering it into the system. It also caused problems in the warehouse because the orders usually got bulk entered, later in the day, and the warehouse staff didn't always have a chance to get the orders pulled and packaged before the delivery trucks picked up for the night. The warehouse manager and I agreed that the customer service folks should be entering the orders into the system as they took them over the phone. When I "introduced" this change to the customer service staff, they weren't as excited as I'd hoped they'd be, leading me to believe that they didn't "see" the benefits. I told them it would be just like ordering something from a catalog and asked them how many had ordered from a catalog over the phone. None had. So, the next day, I placed a catalog order on a speakerphone in the office with my whole staff sitting around listening. The sales rep on the call did up-selling, told us when product would be available, when it would be shipped, and gave us the total cost. When we hung up the phone, I could literally see the light bulbs going off over everyone's head – they finally "saw" what it meant to enter orders online and the benefits in it. The "selling" of the goal was done in the span of two days – Day 1 to figure out they didn't "see" it the way I did and Day 2 to "show" them what it meant so everyone could "see" and strive for the same goal.

Bottom line: Make the end result something that everyone can see and understand, no matter what their job is, and make sure all the goals are aligned to the corporate goals.

Chapter 25

YOUR JOB IS TO GUIDE WITHOUT DOING

YOUR JOB AS a leader is to guide without doing. Once a goal has been set, it is your job, as a leader, to empower your staff to achieve that goal. What empowering your employees really means is to support your people while they do their job. That means:

1. Provide the framework for the goal and what the end result should look like.
2. Set expectations for timeframes, budget constraints, etc…
3. Ask what barriers are in the way and work to remove them.
4. GET OUT OF THE WAY!

While these four steps may seem simplified, they're the basis of what good leaders do. Setting the framework and end result expectation as well as removing identified barriers is what your job is! The hardest part for many leaders, though, is to get out their employees' way. This is especially hard for control freaks, as they believe they should have their hand in and on everything their people do. They want to know every detail and want constant status reports. What this does, however, is create an environment of micromanagement that most good employees don't want any part of – especially the really talented, creative ones – because they aren't being valued for the skills and talents they have. Most of all, that micromanagement makes your employees feel like they're being treated like children. As a leader, you certainly need to have a grasp of what's going on so that you can answer to your management chain, and if you've developed trust with your staff, they'll want to keep you informed, but your true job is to remove the barriers they identify and get out of their way and stay out of their way. Again, this is really hard for control freaks and those leaders who think they have or should have all the answers, but trust me, you'll get SO MUCH MORE from your staff if you empower them and get out their way. They'll feel respected as valued workers and adults and be willing to do much more and go the distance than if they have you looking over their shoulder every step of the way.

Bottom Line: Provide the framework and support, then get out of your people's way and let them do their job.

Chapter 26

HAVE AN "OPEN DOOR POLICY"

THIS A LOADED cliché for many leaders, as they believe they have an "Open Door Policy" because they leave their door open. But the message they send by what they do when an employee comes to talk to them is a whole other story! An "Open Door Policy" means that anyone can come talk to you at anytime and more importantly, that you listen! But it's not as easy as leaving your door open – you have to follow "the rules":

1. When someone asks to talk to you, make time for her, even if you have to schedule it later in the day or the next day. Ask her how long she thinks you'll need together, and then schedule yourself for that amount of time. Don't roll your eyes, or act like it's an imposition or inhale deeply as you look at your watch. That says "I don't have time for you!"

2. Shut the door when you're talking to someone. Make sure you keep any confidences that she's asked of you. If it's information that must be shared, make sure you tell her how much you have to divulge, and if you have to name her to someone, make sure you get her OK first.

3. IGNORE ALL THE OTHER GADGETS AND COMMUNICATION DEVICES IN YOUR OFFICE – Pay attention to the person sitting in front of you. Eyes flitting to a computer screen, your blackberry pinging and getting your attention, or your phone ringing while you're talking to someone is NOT paying attention! Put your phone on call forward or have your calls held. If you can't stop looking at your computer screen, then turn the screen away from your sight or come around the other side of the desk. Put your blackberry on vibrate and in a drawer. Whatever you do – Make the person FEEL like you're listening – and THEN LISTEN!

4. Thank your employee for coming to talk to you. Make sure she knows that she is your job – not an interruption to your job!

5. Follow up on what you agree to do.

A way that I tried to provide an "Open Door Policy" was by giving each person on my staff my business card with the following "coupon" hand-written on the back:

> The card entitles the bearer to one half hour of my time
> May be used repeatedly
> No expiration date
> And then I signed it

It was amazing how many times someone would come into my office and hand me the card as their way of telling me they wanted to talk. You can do whatever works for you, but make sure your staff knows that you're there for them. The information you can get and relationships you can forge and foster through this practice are immeasurable.

Bottom Line: Make sure your employees know they can come talk to you and then follow the 5 rules above.

Chapter 27

Don't Give People Blanks!

PEOPLE FILL IN any blanks they are given – usually with much more negative information than is true, so the simple solution is – DON'T GIVE PEOPLE BLANKS. It is a very painful lesson to learn, but people will ALWAYS fill in any blanks that they are given with much more dire information than is the reality of the situation. Remember, that although you've had many meetings and spent many hours on something, your staff has not. (See Chapter 17 and always "Err on the side of Over-Communication") They don't "know what you know", but you must "know what they don't know". Figure out where the blanks are and help fill them in. Encourage them to ask questions, speak up and speak the truth! If you've already created an environment where it's OK to ask questions, your job will be much easier because they'll tell you the blanks they have.

Along those same lines, remember that everything that is or is not said, sends a message. If you say there will be no layoffs this month, don't think everyone's going to rush up and thank you – all you've done is left a big blank regarding layoffs next month, and that's exactly what people will "want" to believe based on what you haven't said.

Basically, you need to "call a spade a spade" – don't sugarcoat the nasty stuff! Then encourage working through the negatives! They're always there hidden among the "blanks" so it's best to get people to confront reality than to pretend they're not filling in their own blanks to create a negative reality. This way you get to dispel rumors and set the record straight rather than fix problems created by false or lack of information and the rumors they spawn.

Talk plainly and honestly and don't use buzzwords to avoid the ugly truth. Your people know when you're bluffing and when you're not being realistic or telling the whole story. By not being truthful, you leave lots of room for rumor and innuendo. By being honest and over-communicating so that there are no blanks, you can better encourage your folks to be honest and tell you the truth and then you can all confront the truth and find a way to move forward together with an agreed upon acknowledgement of the reality as it is now, filling in the blanks along the way.

Bottom Line: *Give people as much information as possible and don't leave blanks for them to fill in themselves. Encourage them to ask questions so you can fill in the blanks they do have.*

Chapter 28

WALK THE WALK AND TALK THE TALK!

DON'T EXPECT YOUR people to do things you won't or don't do. You have to WALK THE WALK AND TALK THE TALK! Hypocrites and "That is Beneath Me" types aren't good leaders! Make sure that your expectations of your people are not different from those they can expect of you. Don't ever assume, as a leader, that you're above anything. You will destroy your credibility by creating a "class" system that makes you "above" them, because it will make you "above it all" and unapproachable. The more distance you put between yourself and your staff by the things you won't do or don't do will be the measure of how much harder it is to establish an open and productive work environment.

I worked at a small company that owned and managed the building it shared with two other tenants. Things like replacing burnt out light bulbs, stocking toilet paper, and yes, even plunging toilets, could just as easily be handled by me, the Office Manager, as someone else – not always, but enough so that I wasn't "above" anyone or doing anything it took to get the job done.

As a negative example: I once worked with a woman who came to me one day in a rage. She was the support person for a group of "professionals". On this particular day, she came to her desk to find a note attached to a single piece of paper, asking her to make a copy and then put the original and copy on the requestor's desk. It obviously took the requestor more time to write the note than it would have taken to make the copy herself. Any trust and credibility the requestor had ever had with this woman went right out the window – and word of that kind of behavior gets around.

Make sure you're the type of leader who is willing to roll your sleeves up with your employees and get the job done. You'll reinforce that you're all on the same team and reinforce the trust you have already built with them.

Bottom line: Don't expect your employees to do something you don't or won't do and don't ever think you're above doing what it takes to get the job done.

Chapter 29

IF AT FIRST YOU DON'T SUCCEED, TRY, TRY AGAIN!

THE REALITY IS this – there is no perfect way to do or communicate anything. So if you find that you're not getting the results that you want or expect, regroup and try another method of communication. If the goal isn't being met, then talk to folks about what's not working: maybe the end-result goal isn't clear enough; maybe the goal seems too lofty or unattainable or the goals aren't aligned; maybe the result is unrealistic and needs to be modified. Whatever the case, you need to regroup with the your team and try something else. It all revolves around communicating with your staff.

Once you've gotten to the bottom of the issue, make sure you give something time to correct itself or work through before you declare it as not working and then change things again. Changes in direction made too quickly – meaning it may take some time to see the right result and that time hasn't yet passed – can be very debilitating to your staff and not productive to your bottom line.

Keep the communication lines open and keep asking for feedback and the truth. Positively reward those employees giving that honest feedback, because it's invaluable to keeping you and your team moving forward.

Keep communicating with your staff, and you'll keep yourself and them in the loop and keep yourselves on track.

Keep communicating…..see the communication pattern here?!

Bottom Line: If something isn't working the way you expected, keep communicating with your staff about what's not working – keep the communication lines open.

Chapter 30

CELEBRATE SUCCESS AND SUCCESSES!

CELEBRATE YOUR GROUP's success and successes along the way and find ways to thank your employees. There is nothing like a celebration, no matter how big or small to say "thank you" and make people feel good about what they've done and want to do it again. Make a big deal out of the things that go right and make a huge deal out of huge efforts that should be celebrated.

Make sure the celebration fits the effort and sacrifice that went into the success. If your group finished a long-term project on time and/or on budget, then make sure the celebration is big enough to show your appreciation. If the sacrifices were huge and the celebration is small, your staff will feel as if you really don't appreciate the sacrifices they made. I worked for a very large company on a long-term project that required long hours, lots of travel, and conference calls at all hours of the day and night for weeks on end. When the first "milestone" of the project went live, there was a big celebration and everyone felt really good about having achieved the goal. However, as the project dragged on (for several years) and the sacrifices became expected as the norm, the "celebrations" became a painful reminder of how little the company thought of what we did and how much we put into the project, and how the sacrifices were now expected.

Also, while celebrations are important, little things that you can "give" employees are also a big boost to morale. Working a day from home or an extra day off, doesn't really cost the company much if anything and can go a long way to saying "thank you" at the individual employee level.

Ask your staff how they'd like to celebrate the successes or be rewarded. Get them involved in the planning and hosting of the celebration. It's a great way to ensure the success of the celebration and get your staff more involved and own their own success. They will have some great ideas on meaningful ways to celebrate and thank them, that you might never have thought of. Give them a budget, then let them go!

Bottom Line: Celebrate successes, making sure the size of the celebration aligns with the scope of the success. Get your employees involved in the planning and the hosting as well as with ideas on what they consider worthy celebrations and rewards.

DON'T WAIT – DO IT NOW!

NOW THAT YOU have 30 concepts of leadership that you can work on and things you can do to make you a better leader, go out and use them now! Don't wait for the first of the month, the new quarter, a new employee to start, the next meeting, or whatever excuse you want to dream up – Do it now!

Take one or two things and implement them and see how it goes. Then add another and another. Tell your employees you're working on these things and see how positive a response you get and how much they want to help you – they will figure out pretty quickly that it's in their best interest to help you be a better leader and you may be surprised at how many of them are very willing to help. Because in helping you, they'll be helping themselves. You may even see a side of your employees that you've never seen (and you like) and they'll see a side of you they've never seen (and will like). Your team will be more productive, problems will be solved more quickly or won't even materialize because you've created an environment that empowers your staff to work through things and bring them to you before they become problems at all.

Be honest with yourself as you work these concepts. Maintain your honesty and integrity with yourself and everyone you come in contact with. I know that if you take these chapters and honestly incorporate them into your way of operating as a leader, you will grow and experience success as a leader. Have faith in yourself and your team as these changes take shape and as your character as a leader unfolds. This is a great journey that has many rewards along the way. Enjoy them all and share those that you think will help others as the true mark of a leader is how she shares herself with those around her and brings everyone along the successful road she travels.

The Heart of a Leader

Certificate of Completion

YES, I'VE READ THE BOOK!

YES, I'M WORKING ON IT!

THANK YOU FOR YOUR SUPPORT AND SUGGESTIONS!